P9-DHT-452

afternoon
tea

afternoon
tea

jane pettigrew

Publication in this form copyright © Pitkin Publishing 2004,
latest reprint 2011
Text copyright © Jane Pettigrew
The moral right of the author has been asserted
Series editor Jenni Davis
Designed by Mark Buckingham
Pictures researched by Jenni Davis

A CIP catalogue for this book is available from the British Library.

Available by mail order.
See our website, **www.pitkin-guides.com**,
for our full range of titles, or contact us for a copy of our brochure.
Pitkin Publishing
Healey House, Dene Road, Andover, Hampshire, SP10 2AA
Sales and enquiries: 01264 409200
Fax: 01264 334110
Email: sales@thehistorypress.co.uk

Printed in China
ISBN 978-1-84165-143-9   4/11

contents

introduction

Afternoon tea is a ritual to make much of – dressing elegantly for the occasion and using the prettiest china puts the icing on the cake.

Those of us who grew up in families where afternoon tea was regularly served with all the traditional ritual and ceremony will readily understand the charm and appeal of this very British social occasion. Others – who have more recently discovered tea – are constantly delighted and amazed at the unexpected pleasure and joy that tea brings into their lives. For tea is not simply a beverage – it is an essential part of our social life that links us back to ancient China, adds the colour and beauty of fine tea wares to our tables, offers us a drink that is cleansing and revitalizing, and reminds us of the mystical Zen Buddhist powers of tea to calm and focus us in our busy everyday lives. It is, quite simply, the best drink of the day.

setting the scene

Tea should never be taken for granted as an everyday commodity. The story of its discovery in China, its journey into neighbouring countries and more distant lands, its place today in almost every region of the world

and the etiquette and rituals that surround it give it a very special place in our lives.

Various legends attempt to explain the discovery of tea's magical curative powers. The Indians and the Japanese both claim that it was Bodhidharma, a Buddhist priest and founder of Zen Buddhism, who first realized the plant's ability to refresh and restore. The Indian legend tells how the holy man was in the fifth year of a seven-year sleepless meditation when he began to feel drowsy. He plucked a few leaves from a nearby bush, chewed them and was soon once again wide awake. The bush was, of course, a wild tea bush. The Japanese tell how the same priest grew so angry at his eyelids for drooping and almost closing in sleep that he plucked them off and cast them to the ground. Immediately two tea bushes grew up and the leaves were attributed with the power to enhance concentration and restore wakefulness.

But the truth is to be found in China, where the plant is said to have been recognized as possessing the

ability to 'diminish the desire for sleep' as long ago as 2737 BC. Through the ages of ancient dynasties, tea became the drink of the workers as well as the prized luxury of emperors. At court, elegant and refined ritualized contests were held to find the true experts who could recognize different varieties. In the cities, poets and musicians sang the praises of tea as a drink whose 'delicate bitterness reminds one of the taste left by good advice'.

Today, each tea-drinking nation has its own practices and approaches, but none should forget the origins of a drink that spans a 5,000-year history.

the discovery of tea

The Chinese passion for tea is illustrated in this detail of a vase from the Ming Dynasty (1368–1644), showing men watering tea plants. Shen Nung (above) discovered the benefits of tea more than 5,000 years ago.

The health-giving, refreshing and restorative powers of the tea plant, botanically known as *Camellia sinensis*, were first discovered by the mythical Chinese emperor-herbalist Shen Nung. He encouraged the Chinese people to cultivate the plant and drink the infusion of its leaves every day.

Known as the 'Elixir of Life', tea was drunk as a life-enhancing medicinal tonic that could cure ill health and lengthen life. Scholars, priests and monks often lived solely on tea, which helped them to concentrate on their studies and stay awake during long periods of meditation and prayer. Others – with more indulgent tastes – drank tea as a cure for the unpleasant effects of consuming rather too much alcohol, while among the general population tea provided an excellent source of nourishment and sustenance during periods of famine.

But the most important aspect of tea drinking was its role in the social life of the Chinese people. One tea lover from the Song Dynasty (AD 960–1279) explained that 'the proper enjoyment of tea can only be developed in an atmosphere of leisure, friendship and sociability' – a sentiment that is just as relevant a thousand years later.

'Tea gives vigour to the body, contentment to the mind and determination of purpose.'

Shen Nung

tea's arrival in europe

Catherine of Braganza, painted c.1660, shortly before her arrival in England. A poster dating from c.1870 for the East India Tea Company (above).

With increasing contact in the 16th and 17th centuries between China and Europe, as explorers and inquisitive travellers searched the world for new experiences, tales about tea rippled gradually out to new consumers. As the East India Companies of the major European countries vied for Oriental trading rights and domination of the high seas, it was the Dutch and the Portuguese who, in the early 1600s, first brought home a supply of both black and green tea. Small quantities of the costly and unusual herb reached the homes of royal families and wealthy aristocrats around Europe, arriving eventually in London in the late 1650s. Its slow progress was encouraged by Thomas Garraway, a general merchant, who advertised it as a healing tonic that would cure almost all common maladies. His commercial zeal found unexpected support when Catherine of Braganza, a tea-drinking Portuguese princess, arrived in England to marry Charles II in 1662. She had taken the wise precaution of bringing a small supply of tea with her from Portugal, and offered the brew to her friends at court, thus gradually giving the drink a certain upper-class cachet and making it attractively fashionable.

The future of tea was secure.

'Wouldn't it be dreadful to live in a country where they didn't have tea?'

Noel Coward (1899–1973)

early tea-drinking rituals

An English family at tea; painted in the early 18th century by Richard Collins. A selection of tea equipage (above) made in silver and wood by Paul de Lamerie (1688–1751).

japanned caskets and displayed in the 'closet' – a small room next to or near the bedchamber, where valued guests were entertained.

The only role of the servant was to arrange the furniture, set out the tea equipage on a small tea table and to bring a supply of hot water from the kitchens. The lady or gentleman of the house then assumed full responsibility for boiling the water in a silver kettle, carefully measuring the tea into the tiny Chinese earthenware or porcelain teapot, pouring on the boiling water and serving the infusion elegantly into the thimble-sized bowls from which the tea was sipped. Little chunks of sugar were offered on a porcelain dish, delicately dropped into the tea with silver sugar tongs and blended in with small silver teaspoons. Thin slices of bread and butter were offered as the only accompaniment to the brew.

As an exotic and rare commodity, tea very quickly became the costly indulgence of European royal families and aristocrats and so also acquired close associations with palaces and stately homes, elegant and fashionable members of polite society, exquisite porcelains and silverwares, and fine living. Too expensive to leave in the care of the servants, the loose leaf was stored in Chinese porcelain jars or

17th- and 18th-century tea wares

Tea production in a bustling Chinese port, by George Chinnery (1774–1852); an early 18th-century Chinese porcelain tea service painted with peonies (above); an English silver creamer, made by John Schuppe and hallmarked 1758–9.

The ships that carried tea from the South China Seas to the ports of Amsterdam, Lisbon and London also brought the table wares that were essential to the correct preparation and service of the infusion. The name of the country of origin of all the new pots and bowls, saucers and dishes now became a part of the English language as 'cheyney', 'chenea', 'chiney' and 'cheney'. And the tea equipage that appeared on 17th-century tables was not specially designed to suit a new European craze, but was imported and later copied from originals from the Orient.

Teapots were tiny – not, as has been suggested, because the tea was so expensive, but because that is how they were crafted and used by the Chinese. The delicate, translucent tea bowls, without handles, held a mere two or three elegant mouthfuls because

that was the preferred size in China. The flat-sided tea jars that graced the mantelshelves and tabletops of the wealthy had evolved from containers once used by the Chinese to store oil – their little pull-off, push-on caps were ideal for measuring out just the right amount of leaf. Porcelain plates became sugar dishes, and delicate English silver teaspoons, sugar tongs and ornate kettles were added to the necessary equipment to ensure the efficient – but charming – service of tea.

the chinese camellia

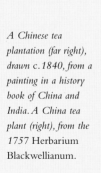

A Chinese tea plantation (far right), drawn c.1840, from a painting in a history book of China and India. A China tea plant (right), from the 1757 Herbarium Blackwellianum.

More than 3,000 different types of tea are made from the leaf buds and leaves of the tea plant, a Camellia that thrives in hot, high and humid conditions. Its delicate white flowers are much smaller than the impressive blooms of the ornamental Camellias and its fruit is a small, hard, oily 'nut', which has an unpleasant bitter taste. If left to its own devices, the Camellia can reach a height of 10m (30ft) or more; for commercial purposes, however, bushes are generally pruned to waist level to ease the job of the pickers.

During the years of China's Tang Dynasty (AD 618–907), the rules for plucking the fragile buds and leaves were strict. Only young unmarried girls were chosen for the skilled task – their hands had to be scrupulously clean; their nails were kept at just the right length for snapping off each new shoot; their diet was free from onions and other strongly flavoured foods, in case the odour was imparted to the tea; and in some cases their fingers were clad in fine silk gloves that covered the hand but left the perfect nails exposed. To ensure the purity of the leaf, each picker would rinse her fingers from time to time in a little jug of water that hung at her waist.

tea in our lives

An illustration by Kate Greenaway of three ladies taking tea on the lawn, in the Girl's Own Annual, 1886. A lady adds sugar to her tea with tongs (above), from the Girl's Own Paper, 24 November 1900.

For quite a few years, following the Second World War, traditional tea-drinking rituals fell by the wayside. Then, in the early 1980s, the first evidence of a tea renaissance became apparent, and not only in the United Kingdom but also in North America, Japan and now all over Europe.

Why has tea once again become so popular among different nationalities and across different age groups? Clearly, one reason is the fact that tea is widely recognized as a healthy, clean and refreshing beverage, the perfect alternative to coffee, alcohol and carbonated soft drinks.

But added to that is the historical link with Oriental tea drinking of almost 5,000 years ago and our own personal nostalgia for tea parties of days gone by, with their associations of comfort and serenity, security and calm. And perhaps the most important

of its benefits today is an almost subconscious awareness of the 'Zen' of tea — the sense that the preparation of the tea wares, the careful and focused brewing of the leaf, the courteous offering and the harmonious sharing of the infusion creates a peaceful space in our pressurized and often frantic lives.

'… sheltered homes and warm firesides — firesides that were waiting — waiting, for the bubbling kettle and the fragrant breath of tea.'

Agnes Repplier, *To Think of Tea*

everything stops for tea

From the earliest days of tea-drinking in Britain, the social gathering of friends and family around the tea table signified an important pause from other daily activities. The event was not a time for business or political

discussions or for dealings involving property or money, but rather a time for refined conversation and light-hearted chatter. Grand ladies and gentlemen ensured that their houses were equipped with all the necessary porcelain bowls, saucers, teapots and dishes from China and Japan, and European or English silver kettles, teaspoons and sugar tongs. Those seeking recognition and prestige among the upper classes knew the importance of owning the finest of tea wares and the latest in tea tables and

trays, for these occasions were wrapped in social significance and revealed much about wealth, taste and status.

In Georgian times, when the wealthy regularly took themselves off for cures in the spa towns and watering holes around the country, tea again provided a break in the routine of promenading, listening to concerts, soaking in a hot pool, playing cards and gambling. In London, the pleasure gardens at Marylebone, Vauxhall, Chelsea and Sadler's Wells attracted people from all classes and walks of life, who relished the chance of a rest from daily toil and an opportunity to take tea in one of the arbours, boxes or tea houses that always featured at these venues.

In time, the taste for tea filtered down to the poorer members of society, who also took to little 'tea breaks' both for refreshment and as a chance to gossip with friends and workmates. In rural areas, the constant demand of household chores was alleviated when women gathered together to sip tea and enjoy a short break. Out in the fields, labourers sought respite from the relentless summer sun and settled in the shade of a haystack to drink tea from the bottles and mugs carried out to them by the farmer's wife.

Today, it is still the same. At home or work, for a group of friends or a person alone – when a break is needed, tea provides the perfect refreshment.

the beginning of afternoon tea

A portrait of Anna Maria, 7th Duchess of Bedford, in coronation robes. An early 19th-century hot-water jug and kettle (above and right), such as the duchess might have used when serving tea.

The innovation of the mid-afternoon indulgence called 'afternoon tea' is accredited to Anna Maria, 7th Duchess of Bedford. In fact, she did not 'invent' the ceremony, but simply gave it a name that settled it as a four o'clock social occasion at a time when the pattern of mealtimes was changing.

When tea first arrived in England in the mid-17th century, it was taken as a settler at the end of dinner, a large, heavy meal that lasted four or five hours from noon to late afternoon. By the early years of the 19th century, this huge meal had shifted to around 7.30pm or even later, leaving a long gap between breakfast and the evening repast. Only light refreshment was provided at midday by the newly invented luncheon, or 'noonshine'.

And so the Duchess found it pleasing and convenient to serve tea two or three hours before dinner, as well as (or instead of) after the meal. Indeed, Anna Maria found 'afternoon tea' so essential to her daily routine that when she visited friends in their castles and palaces, she took with her a silver kettle and other tea equipage along with her trunks and hat boxes.

'Tea's proper use is to amuse the idle, and relax the studious, and dilute the full meals of those who cannot use exercise, and will not use abstinence.'

Samuel Johnson (1709–84)

choosing the leaf

The most wonderful thing about tea is the wide choice of flavours and aromas offered by more than 35 tea-producing countries. All teas – green, white, oolong, black, flavoured, compressed – are made from the versatile *Camellia sinensis*, and it is the different growing conditions and the varying methods of manufacture that give rise to the wide range. For those who prefer the lightest of liquors and the most delicate of flavours, there are exquisitely pale white teas and soft smooth greens from China; herby, almost fishy greens from Japan; light and sappy first- and second-flush teas from Darjeeling; and subtle, peach-flavoured oolongs from Taiwan. Those who love a strong, dark, pungent brew choose the rich, black teas of Africa, the golden briskness of Ceylons, and the malty, smooth strength of Assams.

Traditional 'orthodox' teas are shown more respect during the manufacturing procedure and the larger pieces of leaf give a more subtle quality to the infusion. Teas made for tea-bag blends are reduced to tiny particles that brew quickly and conveniently and give a darker, more coppery liquid.

Choose stronger teas to complement richer foods and the more subtle green teas to accompany Oriental foods, sushi and Thai noodles. As with wines, different teas marry well with different foods and it is only by tasting them together that personal choices develop.

Different types of tea produce a brew that varies remarkably in colour – the darker the tea, the stronger the taste.

26

brewing the perfect cup of tea

Tea must be carefully stored in an airtight container that protects the leaf from light, humidity and contaminating odours, and guards its freshness and quality. Fill the kettle with fresh cold water to ensure that plenty of oxygen bubbles through it. Stale, reboiled water makes flat, lifeless tea. While the water boils, gather together a teapot of an appropriate size, a caddy spoon to measure the leaf, the caddy of tea, a digital timer, a bone china or porcelain cup and saucer, and – if required – milk and sugar.

The essential ingredients for making a really excellent cup of tea – beautiful bone china, a digital timer, a caddy spoon and a tea strainer.

When the water is boiling, pour a little into the pot, swirl it around and then tip it away. Measure in the correct amount of tea, allowing approximately 2.5g (1 caddy spoon/1½ tsp) for 200ml (½ pint) of water. Pour the boiling water onto the leaves, replace the lid of the pot, set the digital timer and allow to brew for the correct number of minutes. In general, small–leafed black teas need 2–3 minutes; larger leaves need 3–5 minutes and oolong teas need 5–7 minutes. A removable infuser or disposable paper filter allows the leaves to be lifted from the pot at the end of the correct brewing time, so that the tea does not develop a bitter taste. When brewing green tea, allow the boiled water to cool to about 80–85°C (176–185°F) before pouring onto the leaves.

the best teapot

The most suitable vessels in which to prepare tea are made of porcelain, bone china, glazed stoneware, earthenware or glass. Materials to avoid include aluminium, pewter and – despite its elegance and the sense of history it adds to the tea table – silver. Silver looks wonderful but the metal tends to cling to the flavour of the last tea brewed in it and this can taint the next. To avoid this problem, but still enjoy silver's traditional elegance, choose a modern Teflon-lined silver pot for a perfect infusion every time tea is made in it.

The best teapots for brewing perfect tea – fine bone china (far right) and Chinese Yixing pots (above and below right).

Tea connoisseurs love the unglazed earthenware pots from China's Yixing – a lakeside area famed for its coloured clay that is used to fashion exquisite handmade pots in the form of houses, animals, lotus flowers, bundles of bamboo, dragons and other fantasy shapes. Unglazed both inside and out, the pots are said to be better than any other for the respectful and sympathetic brewing of China teas. Each pot should be reserved for brewing only one type of tea, allowing a patina of colour and flavour to develop on the inner surface. As this enhances future brews, the body should never be washed inside, merely rinsed out and left to dry.

from tea bowl to cup and saucer

As with so many contemporary tea wares, the origin of the teacup and saucer can be traced back to ancient China. When the European trading companies began their commerce in tea and tea wares, Oriental tea bowls were (and still are) small, without handles, and designed to offer the drinker a few elegant sips. Originally used without saucers, the little individual rests are thought to have been developed to facilitate the handing around of very hot tea. As the fashion for tea drinking in Britain grew, so the first teacup was created, by adapting the handle from the English posset cup (a tall, straight-sided drinking vessel used to serve hot mulled wines and ales) to the Chinese bowl. The result was still shallow and bowl-shaped, but slightly larger and with its own graciously curving means of protecting fingers from scorching porcelain. With restricted space for fingers and thumbs, the little finger on the hands of well-bred ladies trailed upwards and outwards, away from the rest of the hand, in the classic aristocratic gesture of refinement.

A family taking tea in the mid 18th century – the tray is placed on an elegant little tea table; English tea bowls and saucers, c.1760, in tin-glazed earthenware with Chinese-style decoration and (above) the evolved teacup with a handle.

To indicate that enough tea had now been consumed, a lady would turn her teacup upside down on its saucer or tap it daintily with the teaspoon – whereupon a servant or one of the gentleman present would remove it.

children's tea china

A doll's tea party, an illustration for Frances Hodgson Burnett's classic tale A Little Princess; *nursery tea (above), served on Bunnykins china.*

Throughout the second half of the 19th century and into the 20th, the afternoon tea party became a vital part of British social life, and while mothers in middle- and upper-class homes were entertaining friends and neighbours to tea in the drawing room, their children enjoyed the same ritual up in the nursery with their governess or nanny.

To make the occasion more fun, potteries and porcelain companies started designing some charming and inventive tablewares to appeal to the younger tea drinkers. These were often decorated with favourite characters from children's stories and nursery rhymes – Mickey Mouse, Humpty Dumpty, Winnie the Pooh, Alice in Wonderland, Bunnykins and many of Beatrix Potter's woodland creatures.

Even smaller, miniature teasets were created so that the children might entertain their dolls and teddy bears to afternoon tea – a very important time in any little girl's day.

'Afternoon Tea was a very important business with Ellie. It was generally spread on the floor, and if the tea-things got a bit scattered, it was really not to be wondered at. You see, the dollies wanted such a lot of attention, as they were unable to help themselves, poor things!'

Constance M. Lowe, *Afternoon Tea*

tea gardens and tea shops

The Willow Tea Rooms, Glasgow, illustrated by Dora Holzhandler (1990). 'The Tea-Shop Girl' (above), a postcard produced in 1902. A scene in a tea shop, 1899 (right), from The Book of Shops.

The now-famous tradition of going out to tea dates back to the 1880s in Glasgow, where one Stuart Cranston owned a small tea retail business. Anxious that his customers should be able to taste his teas in comfort before buying, he decided to install a few tables and chairs and offered pots of tea, bread and butter and a small selection of cakes. A few years later, Cranston's sister Kate opened the first of her chain of Art Nouveau-style tearooms, including the famous Willow Tea Rooms, designed by the innovative architect Charles Rennie Mackintosh.

In London, the Aerated Bread Company (ABC) is thought to have been the pioneer of the tea shop in the south when the manageress of its London Bridge branch converted a spare back room into a tearoom where customers could enjoy a refreshing pot of tea with the shop's breads and cakes.

Once the ABC had demonstrated the potential of the public tearoom, other companies seized the opportunity to offer tea as well as the chocolates, milk, tobacco, cakes and other provisions that were their main business.

Out of town, villagers in picturesque parts of the British countryside opened their gardens and front parlours to a growing number of cyclists, walkers and day-trippers who needed some refreshment while out exploring. Soon there were tearooms, tea shops and tea gardens everywhere.

putting on the ritz

The Palm Court of the Ritz Hotel, where afternoon tea is served beautifully; (above) elegant musical entertainment is an added attraction for those taking tea in the Roman-temple-style Pump Room in Bath.

For those occasions when afternoon tea is to be a celebration, there are several gloriously English venues that really do things in style. Among these are the chic Ritz Hotel in London's Piccadilly, the Pump Room in Bath and The National Trust's Waddesdon Manor, Buckinghamshire.

Tea at the Ritz is served at a table perfectly laid with spotless, crisp white linen tablecloth and napkins, fine china with a faintly Oriental air and silver cutlery. The tea arrives in a splendid silver teapot, accompanied by hot water and milk served in silver jugs. A selection of sandwiches is followed by delicious scones – as light as air and topped with home-made strawberry preserve and thick clotted cream – and irresistibly tempting little cakes and pastries. Exquisite!

In the late 18th century, the Pump Room in Bath was the social centre for those taking the spa waters. Today, tea is served in this charming room to the harmonious chords of the Pump Room Trio, the oldest musical ensemble in England. At Waddesdon Manor, a choice of satisfying high teas, celebration champagne teas and children's teas reminiscent of the Victorian nursery are served to visitors in the warm and welcoming ambience of the old kitchen and servants' hall.

tea parties

With the institution of afternoon tea firmly established by the 1860s, the perfect focus for parties had been created in British social life. The tea event was adapted to birthday parties, wedding receptions, Christmas festivities

and other celebrations of all kinds. If the gathering was to be made up of a select few, then tea was served in the drawing room or boudoir. If a larger reception was planned – sometimes for up to 200 people – the ballroom, hall or garden was arranged with long buffet tables covered with crisp white linen cloths, and servants were allocated to different areas to pour tea and hand it around to the guests on trays. Etiquette books advised that: 'Relays of tea, boiling water, and hot buttered toast or muffins must be brought by the servant

as required, with clean cups, and she must bring a tray to remove those that have been used.'

Today's tea parties follow much the same pattern, with celebrations taking place in private houses, in tearooms and in hotel lounges where waiting staff delight in making a fuss of the birthday girl or boy and often bring out a cake on which candles brightly flicker and glow.

The great joy of the tea party is its total flexibility and adaptability to all manner of events, to all types of

people, and to all ages. Tea parties may be themed to suit the season, for example, or the age of the guests, the reason for the celebration, and the taste of those who are participating. Table decorations, china, linens and the food itself can be carefully chosen to add colour and style to the elegance of the traditional tea table and create an event that will always hold a place in the memory of those who were present.

organizing a tea party

Tea in the garden on a perfect summer afternoon is the height of gracious living; pretty china (above) is essential to add a lovely sense of occasion to a tea party.

Following the tradition of Victorian Britain, guests to a tea party should be invited a few days beforehand, either by telephone or by hand-written note. On the day of the party, the hostess must decide where she will hold the gathering – on the terrace, perhaps, or in the garden, or would the drawing room or the conservatory be better suited to the weather? Certainly not in the dining room or kitchen, for tea should always be served in the most gracious part of the house or garden, where armchairs, sofas and chaises longues allow guests to be seated comfortably and elegantly. Small, low tables should be placed close to each seat and a larger table or trolley set ready with all the tea things.

When guests arrive, take their coats, make any necessary introductions and invite people to sit down. When everyone is comfortable and chatting happily together, slip out to the kitchen to make the tea and fetch the food. Give each guest a small plate and a napkin, then pour a cup of tea for each person and hand them around, offering milk and sugar to those who wish to add them to their cup. Then offer all the deliciously tempting edible treats you have chosen to serve.

laying the tea table or trolley

Lloyd Loom chairs around a small wicker-work table make a charming setting for tea; crisp white table linen enhances fresh, flowery china (above).

19th-century tea: 'A small gypsy-table should be kept for the purpose of holding the tea tray, or one of the wicker-work afternoon tea tables, with shelves underneath for the plates of cake and bread-and-butter.' The table or trolley should be set ready with side plates and cups and saucers (which may be stacked neatly to save space), silver teaspoons, a jug of milk, a bowl of sugar cubes with tongs, the pot of tea, a jug of boiling water, a tea strainer on its own little rest or dish, little linen tea napkins, tea knives and pastry forks. As in Victorian times, it is the hostess's responsibility to pour the tea and hand it to her guests, offering also milk and sugar and ensuring that each person has all that he or she requires. Sandwiches, cakes, scones and biscuits may be presented on a folding multi-tier wooden or rattan cake stand positioned near the table.

Afternoon drawing-room tea is traditionally arranged so that guests are seated in armchairs and sofas and have low tables close beside them upon which to set their cup and saucer. The hostess dispenses the tea from a small table or trolley in the manner of a

laying the tea table or trolley

A cake stand is an elegant and eye-catching way to present tea-time treats. A beautiful tray (right) is a very attractive way to present the essential items of a tea-drinking ceremony.

If tea-party guests are to be seated around a table, first cover it with a spotless lace or linen cloth. Place a small vase of flowers in the centre and, at each place, arrange a side plate and place neatly on top of it a small linen napkin and a small tea knife. In front of the hostess's place, set ready mats for the teapot and hot-water jug, cups and saucers, little silver teaspoons, a jug of milk, a bowl of cube sugar (with sugar tongs) and a tea strainer. Around the vase of flowers position a dish of

butter, if needed, with a small butter knife, dishes of jam and whipped or clotted cream, and plates of elegant, crustless sandwiches, scones, crumpets, biscuits and cakes. If space is limited, these look wonderfully attractive and appetizing set on cake stands. Also have ready small silver three-pronged pastry forks so that indulgent pastries and cakes may be enjoyed without fingers becoming embarrassingly sticky.

'There are few hours in life more agreeable than the hour dedicated to the ceremony known as afternoon tea.'

Henry James (1843–1916)

teatime treats

seed cake

170g/6oz/³/₄ cup soft butter
140g/5oz/²/₃ cup caster sugar
2 large eggs, beaten
140g/5oz/1¹/₄ cups
  self-raising flour
60g/2oz/¹/₂ cup plain flour
grated zest and juice
  of one lemon
2tsp caraway seeds
2tbsp demerara sugar,
  to sprinkle

Heat oven to 170°C/325°F/gas mark 3
Grease and base-line an 18cm/7in round cake tin

Sift together the self-raising and plain flour. Beat together the butter and caster sugar until pale and fluffy. Beat in the lemon zest and add the eggs, a little at a time, beating well after each addition. Lightly fold in the sifted flour, lemon juice and caraway seeds. Turn the mixture into the tin, level the surface and sprinkle over the demerara sugar. Bake for about 45 minutes, until the cake is beginning to shrink from the sides of the tin. Cool in the tin for ten minutes, then turn out onto a rack to cool completely. Wrap in foil and store for a day or two before serving.

Old-fashioned favourites for serving with afternoon tea – a lemony seed cake and (below) macaroons.

macaroons

170g/6oz/1²/₃ cups
  ground almonds
3tbsp icing sugar
1tsp ground rice
225g/8oz/1 cup granulated sugar
3 medium egg whites
flaked almonds and caster sugar,
  to sprinkle

Heat oven to 150°C/300°F/gas mark 2
Line 2 baking sheets with rice paper or non-stick baking parchment

Stir together the dry ingredients then mix to a paste with the egg whites. Place generous teaspoons of the mixture well apart on the baking sheets, flatten slightly with the back of a spoon and sprinkle with flaked almonds and caster sugar. Bake for 25–30 minutes, until tinged a light golden brown.
Makes about 24.

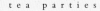
teatime treats

Cold winter days call for warming comfort food – moist gingerbread and (above) date slices fit the bill perfectly.

gingerbread

140g/5oz/generous
  ½ cup butter
375g/13oz/1 cup golden syrup
255g/9oz/2¼ cups
  plain flour
1¾ tsp bicarbonate of soda
½ tsp salt
½ tsp mixed spice
½ tsp cinnamon
2tsp ground ginger
280ml/10fl oz/1¼ cups milk
1 egg

Heat oven to 180°C/350°F/gas mark 4
Grease and base-line an 18–20cm/7–8in square cake tin

Melt the butter and golden syrup together in a pan over a low heat. Sift together the flour, bicarbonate of soda, salt and spices. Beat together the milk and egg. Gradually add the melted butter and syrup to the dry ingredients and mix thoroughly. Gradually add the milk and egg mixture and mix to a smooth and very runny batter. Pour into the tin and bake for 50 minutes, or until a skewer inserted in the middle comes out clean. Leave to cool in the tin for 15 minutes, then turn out onto a rack to cool completely. Wrap in foil and store for a few days before serving.

date slices

225g/8oz/1¾ cups
  dates, chopped
pinch of cinnamon
grated zest and juice of one orange
  (add water to the juice to make
  up to 150ml/5fl oz/1¼ cups)
115g/4oz/1 cup plain flour
170g/6oz/2 cups rolled oats
170g/6oz/1 cup (packed) light
  soft brown sugar
170g/6oz/1 cup butter, melted

Heat oven to 180°C/350°F/gas mark 4
Grease and base-line a shallow, 18cm/7in square tin

Place the dates, cinnamon, orange zest and orange juice in a pan, bring to the boil, cover and cook slowly, stirring occasionally until pulpy (about 6 minutes). Mix together the remaining ingredients. Press half the oat mixture into the base of the tin, spread over the date mixture, and sprinkle with the rest of the oat mixture, pressing it down. Bake for 20 minutes until golden. Cool and cut into squares to serve.
Makes 12 squares.

teatime treats

strawberry amaretto shortcake

No summer afternoon tea is complete without a slice of indulgent strawberry shortcake; toasted crumpets with a generous dollop of butter and some home-made jam are a classic tea-time treat.

75g/2½oz/¾ cup plain flour
75g/2½oz/¾ cup
 ground almonds
3tbsp chopped almonds
75g/2½oz/⅓ cup butter
50g/1¾oz/¼ cup caster sugar
1 egg white
200g/7oz strawberries, sliced
200ml/7fl oz/¾ cup
 double cream
amaretto, to taste
five whole strawberries and icing
 sugar, to decorate

Heat oven to 180°C/350°F/gas mark 4
Line a baking sheet with non-stick baking parchment

Cream the sugar and butter until soft and fluffy. Add the ground almonds and the flour and knead to a dough. Divide the mixture into two and roll out each half on the baking sheet. Cut each piece into a 16cm/6in round. Brush the egg white over one of the rounds and sprinkle with the chopped almonds. Bake for 20 minutes until pale golden. Carefully cut the almond-topped half into quarters, then leave both rounds to cool completely. Reserve a little whipped cream for the decoration. Stir the amaretto into the remaining whipped cream, then gently stir in the strawberries. Coat the whole shortcake round with the mixture, then arrange the shortcake quarters on top. Decorate with the whipped cream and whole strawberries, and top with a sprinkle of icing sugar. Makes 4 slices.

dressing for tea

Tea gowns designed by 'Lucile' (Lady Duff Gordon), 1910 (far right). All dressed up for a garden party (right) – a fashion illustration of 1911.

By the second half of the 19th century, afternoon tea had been established as a very feminine social occasion at which ladies (and sometimes gentlemen too) gathered to gossip and sip tea.

Since the ideal waist size at that time was a mere 45cm (18in) around, participants were often uncomfortably strapped into cruelly tight whalebone corsets. On recognition of the dangers to health of 'tight lacing', a gradual movement to change the way in which ladies dressed led designers to create a looser, kinder style of clothing.

Browsing through the pages of fashion magazines, ladies soon began to find their eyes drawn to pictures of loose, softly flowing tea gowns of satin and lace, chiffon and silk, decorated with bows, ribbons and crystal beads. The idea of the tea gown was that it allowed ladies to leave off their stays, at least for an hour or two between the more formal lunch and dinner, but continue to look ravishingly beautiful and feminine.

Not intended as garments in which to leave the house, these frocks were ideal for tea on the terrace or in the drawing room. Mrs Eric Pritchard, an expert on such matters, understood the importance of soft, luxurious fabrics: 'Let me offer up a thanksgiving to the inventor of chiffon, for without its delusive folds I do not believe we could imagine the tea gown or any garment of this sort ....'

the tea dance

The tango took afternoon tea to a new dimension; here, two elegant couples show how it's done in illlustrations of c.1914.

Victorian tea parties often included some form of entertainment, such as a piano recital, a poetry reading, or perhaps – for the younger, sprightlier members of the group – a dance or two, often referred to as 'dancing on the carpet'; so the idea of mingling tea with dancing was an established idea by the turn of the 20th century. But it was the arrival in London of the tango in 1910 that led to the quirky and slightly eccentric idea of Tango Tea Dances in hotels, clubs and restaurants. By 1913, the afternoon 'Thés Dansants' were quite the most fashionable event on the social calendar, and at the Waldorf Hotel 'little parties of from two to six can sit and enjoy a most excellent tea between the dances ... here tangos are a special feature of the programme, at least six or seven being played ...'.

Special tango tea frocks were designed, moody and seductive music was written for dance bands and singers, professional male dancers were provided at some venues so that ladies who attended without a partner (perfectly acceptable by the rules of contemporary etiquette) might show off their intricate footwork, and daily newspapers carried headlines such as 'Tango Tea for 1,500' and 'Everyone's Tangoing Now'!

children's tea parties

Sir John Tenniel's illustration of The Mad Hatter's Tea Party from Lewis Carroll's fantasy for children, Alice's Adventures in Wonderland. *Iced fairy cakes are a must at a child's tea party.*

In 1889, *Mrs Armstrong's Good Form* told readers: 'The refreshments at a juvenile party should be simple in character, but an abundance of bon-bons is an essential requirement. The children's tea is served soon after their arrival ... with the governess and lady's maid presiding at either side.'

Ever since tea parties became such a favourite social event, birthdays, anniversaries and other special occasions have been celebrated over cups of tea and an array of beautifully presented savoury dishes, elaborate cakes and sweet treats. Over the years, children's birthday parties have been made more lively and colourful with shiny balloons tied to the backs of chairs, bright paper hats for everyone to wear, and food presented in unusual and imaginative ways. The highlight of the meal is the presentation of the birthday cake decorated with the glow of burning candles, the singing of birthday wishes and the ritual blowing-out of the candles.

And then, just as at Victorian tea parties, 'when all the cakes are finished, a general adjournment is made to the drawing-room when the games and dances begin'. Children's parties have always included the fun of old-fashioned 'pass-the-parcel', 'pin the tail on the donkey', 'hide and seek', and entertainment provided by jugglers, puppeteers and magicians who have the children wrapped in silent awe or shrieking with delight.

tea trivia

The world of tea links us by its wider associations to many other areas of fascination and historical interest. Tea cannot be properly enjoyed without also considering the caddy in which it is stored, the pot in which it is

brewed, the cup from which it is drunk, the jug from which the milk is added to the cup and the silver spoon with which the brew is stirred. These objects each inspire thoughts of the originals that arrived from China in the 17th century and of the creative inventions that have appeared on our tea tables ever since.

The acts of brewing and serving tea link us also to the etiquette and manners of the tea party and to the role that tea has played in our social life over the past three and a half centuries.

Taxation severely affected the price and therefore the affordability of tea from the 1660s to the 1860s. Laws were passed to arrest the unacceptable adulteration of tea with other leaves and chemicals. Bitter wars were fought between Britain and China over the trading of tea and opium.

Because tea has, for almost 350 years, been so widely drunk by all classes in all areas of Britain, stories, superstitions and strange beliefs have grown up around it. In some parts of the country, it was once believed that if two women poured from the same teapot, one of them would be sure to fall pregnant and give birth to ginger-haired twins. In some fishing areas on the east coast, the teapot was never emptied on the day the fishing boats set sail in case it emptied the husband out of the house to a watery death.

And tea leaves hold great significance for many who believe that the truth about their future lies hidden in the patterns left by the wet leaves in the bottom of the cup.

The connections and the trivial fascination of tea add to the charm of this timeless beverage.

reading the leaves

Two women try to discover their fate in this painting by Alma Broadbridge. The way the tea leaves settle in the cup (above) gives a message to those who understand their secrets.

For hundreds of years, people have gazed into the pattern of wet tea leaves scattered in the bottom of their cup in order to try and fathom the future. Can this ever be a serious exercise in fortune-telling, or is it simply a little light fun?

Tea expert James Norwood Pratt once wrote: 'Perhaps the best thing to be said for reading tea leaves is that it can be quite thoroughly frivolous from start to finish.' But Amber McCarroll, British Tasseologist, believes that tea-leaf reading 'is an ancient and intuitive experience' that helps us to develop our individual creativity and find a balance between what we know consciously and feel subconsciously.

Whatever the attitude of those taking part, the cup must first be carefully prepared. There must be at least half a teaspoonful of wet leaves and a little liquid in the cup; the upright cup must be turned anticlockwise three times and then tipped upside down onto the saucer. Symbols in the bottom of the cup represent important, serious events and emotions, while the area around the rim holds the more light-hearted images. Look at the contents from all angles and keep an open mind when trying to interpret the shapes you see, for you may just see 'the grounds of fate in grounds of tea'.

tea caddies

An elegant 18th-century caddy fitted with lock and key to confound the servants (far right); a 19th-century caddy in the form of a shoe (right); an 18th-century glass tea caddy with enamel decoration and a pewter lid (below).

The little porcelain jars used to store tea in the 17th century in England gradually lost their elegant narrow necks and neat caps and became squatter, fatter chests and boxes crafted in precious woods, crystal, silver, tortoiseshell and porcelain.

And because the tea was such an expensive luxury, the idea evolved to lock it inside the stylish container so that wealthy householders could keep the tea out of the hands of the servants, who by this time had acquired a taste

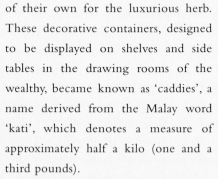

of their own for the luxurious herb. These decorative containers, designed to be displayed on shelves and side tables in the drawing rooms of the wealthy, became known as 'caddies', a name derived from the Malay word 'kati', which denotes a measure of approximately half a kilo (one and a third pounds).

Because ladies liked to keep more than one type of tea in the house and used several jars or boxes to store them, cabinet makers developed larger chests, also lockable, to hold two or three individual containers for tea and equally expensive lump sugar. At tea-time, as in earlier years, the servant would arrange the furniture and tea equipage, but it was the host or hostess who took down the caddy from its prominent position in the drawing room, unlocked it and proceeded to conduct the tea-brewing ceremony.

65

tea and health

*Cyclists radiate the good
health and happiness
that go hand-in-hand
with getting plenty of
fresh air and exercise
and drinking tea.*

Stories about tea arriving from China in the 17th century told of the drink's almost miraculous ability to cure everyday ailments, maintain health and prolong life. The first advertisement in London claimed that tea could cure – among many other maladies – stomach upsets, skin complaints, memory loss, headaches and breathing problems.

Recent research has proved that at least some of those unsubstantiated claims are indeed true and it is now believed that tea can help protect us against certain cancers, heart attacks, strokes, thrombosis, high levels of cholesterol and hardening of the arteries. And of course tea is an excellent way to keep our daily fluid intake topped up, ensuring that we do not become dehydrated, tired and prone to headaches.

Tea works for the good of our health from inside the body, but it can work its magic from the outside, too. The world of cosmetics now offers tea-based skin-care products – anti-ageing moisturizers, wrinkle-banishing creams, cleansing shampoos, protective sun blocks, invigorating scrubs, energizing bath oils and perfumes, adding yet another dimension to the power of tea.

*'If you are cold,
  tea will warm you;
If you are too heated,
  it will cool you;
If you are depressed,
  it will cheer you;
If you are exhausted,
  it will calm you.'*

William Gladstone (1809–98)

early tea advertising

In 1658, the first advertisement for tea in *Mercurius Politicus*, a local London newspaper, announced the public sale of 'That excellent and by all Physitians approved, China Drink'. Two years later, Thomas Garraway told readers of his broadsheet on tea that 'The said Leaf is of such known virtues, that those very nations so famous for Antiquity, Knowledge and Wisdom frequently sell it among themselves for twice its weight in silver'.

By the end of the 17th century, an essay by J. Ovington claimed that the drink was excellent against 'Diabetes, cholick, stone, gravel, dropsy and weakness of the sight' and encouraged the consumption of tea as a healthy alternative to alcohol.

In the early years of the 19th century, tea prices began to drop after years of heavy taxation and, with an ever-increasing number of merchants competing for customers, it was important to offer something extra. John Horniman offered 'Pure Tea' in guaranteed weights inside foil-lined bags. Later in the century, the London Tea Company advertised its products as 'Lovely Tea, suitable for Five o'clock Tea'. Thomas Lipton advertised his Ceylon teas as 'Direct from the tea garden to the teapot', while his competitors offered free pensions, guidebooks, teapots, linens and even pianos in exchange for coupons cut carefully from tea packets.

A Victorian tradecard advertising Horniman's Pure Tea; a waitress in the distinctive black uniform of Lyons' Tea Houses – the first was opened in 1894.

LYONS' TEA

tea and temperance

A scene from the Charles Dickens' classic, Pickwick Papers. *Mr Stiggins (seated) is the drunken leader of London's Brick Lane Temperance Movement – regrettably not a shining example! Temperance propaganda, such as this 1870 postcard (below), made its message very clear.*

With a growing recognition of the very great evils and dangers of heavy alcohol consumption, the Temperance Movement was founded in the 1820s to encourage those who indulged in ale, wine, beer, whisky, gin and rum to try a healthier, cleaner drink – tea. In 1827, W. Newnham wrote that 'green tea is found to be particularly useful in the headache produced by the stimulation of alcoholic fluids' and 'teetotallers' were helped in their mission to convert drunkards by the general acceptance that tea was actually a very healthy alternative to all those harmful beverages.

For some reason, the movement took particular hold in Preston and set a trend for temperance tea parties when it entertained 1,200 non-drinkers to an alcohol-free Christmas celebration. The food was donated by local people and 'about forty men, principally reformed drunkards, were busily engaged as waiters, water-carriers, etc; those who waited at table wore white aprons with "temperance" printed on the front'.

William Carter wrote in his book, *The Power of Truth*, that more than 70 'extraordinary tea meetings' had been held for different groups since his book had appeared in 1865. He reckoned that, with 400–500 people at each of those meetings, more than 30,000 converts had been drawn into the movement through the power of tea.

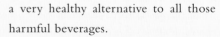

tea cosies

A fabulously ornate crinoline-lady tea cosy; a silk-lined linen canvas tea cosy decorated with tassels and glass beads (above); and a modern tea cosy (right) that looks good enough to wear to Ladies' Day in Royal Ascot Week.

When the Victorians made tea time such an important part of their social life, they very sensibly developed a means of keeping the tea as hot as possible for as long as possible. Drawing rooms in those days did not benefit from the luxury of central heating, and food and drink cooled much more quickly than today.

How sensible, then, to envelop the teapot in its own thickly padded jacket. With the Victorian love of elaborate ornamentation and decoration, the often simple form of the cosy became the focus of intricate embroidery, lace trimmings, colourful tassels, beading and other embellishments.

Most cosies could be popped easily over the teapot after the tea had been poured, but others were fashioned rather like handbags that could be pulled up and around the pot to encase it totally. Gradually, the idea evolved of providing little holes for spout and handle so that the cosy could remain safely in place while the tea was being dispensed, and the consequent ease of pouring led to its nickname – the 'bachelor' tea cosy. But probably the quirkiest of cosies were the dainty 'crinoline ladies' that sat pertly over the teapot, their porcelain bodies attached to brightly coloured knitted or crocheted skirts whose layers kept the tea hot.

milk in first?

Adding the milk to the cup before pouring in the tea may allow the two liquids to blend more efficiently, but is it good etiquette?

And now we come to the perennial problem that faces all dedicated tea drinkers – the question of the right moment to add milk to the tea.

Although there is little evidence of milk being taken in tea during the first 50 or so years of tea drinking in England, it has since become a popular and accepted addition in the British tea cup. And ever since the practice began, the debate has run and run as to whether the milk should be poured into the cup before the tea or the tea before the milk. Some claim that it was always added to the bowl before the boiling tea to protect the paper-thin porcelain from the risk of shattering. Victorian etiquette demanded that milk or cream should be offered after the cups of tea had been handed to guests by their hostess.

Modern 'milk-in-first' tea drinkers argue that their preferred ritual gives a better mixing of the two liquids, while the 'milk-in-second' brigade believe that by pouring the milk into the tea, one has a better chance of getting the proportions correct for strength and colour. Scientists support the M-I-F theory and advise that, by adding cold milk to boiling hot tea, there is a slight chance of scalding the fat content in the milk and thus possibly changing the overall flavour of the tea.

The final choice, however, in this critical matter, must be that of each individual tea drinker!

the simplicity of tea

The legend 'A lovely pot of tea' on this modern teapot sums up the sentiments of all dedicated tea-drinkers.

In today's fast-moving and often frantic life, pausing to take afternoon tea offers a brief but valuable respite from everyday pressures; so let all tea drinkers turn to the steadying influence of the tea 'ceremony'. Let us all discover how the ritual of carefully gathering together all the beautiful and fascinating objects needed for the perfect brewing and serving of tea can centre and calm us. Carried out with thoughtful attention to detail and consideration of the style and mood required for any one occasion or any particular group of people, the preparation and sharing of a cup of tea reminds us of our links with the past, of the ancient cultures and of the importance of recognizing and appreciating the innate beauty to be found in such simple actions.

'Teaism is a cult founded on the adoration of the beautiful among the sordid facts of everyday existence. It inculcates purity and harmony, the mystery of mutual charity, the romanticism of the social order ... Let us have a sip of tea. Let us dream of evanescence, and linger in the beautiful foolishness of things.

Okakura Kakuzo, *Book of Tea*

places to visit

The following are some of the best tearooms around Britain:

ABBEY COTTAGE TEA ROOMS
26 Main Street, New Abbey, Dumfries; Tel 01387 850377
A delightful tearoom in a 19th-century cottage.

BADGER'S CAFÉ & PATISSERIE
The Victoria Centre, Mostyn Street, Llandudno; Tel 0192 871649
A Victorian atmosphere in a modern shopping mall.

BETTY'S CAFÉ TEAROOMS
1 Parliament Street, Harrogate, North Yorkshire; Tel 01423 877300
Famous tearooms with a comfortable, traditional feel.

BIRD ON THE ROCK TEAROOM
Abcott, Clungunford, Shropshire; Tel 01588 660631
Enchanting tearooms designed and run in 1930s style.

ELIZABETH BOTHAM & SONS
35/39 Skinner Street, Whitby, North Yorkshire; Tel 01947 602823
Tearooms above a bakery run by the same family since 1865.

THE HAZELMERE CAFÉ & BAKERY
1 Yewbarrow Terrace, Grange over Sands, Cumbria; Tel 01539 532972
Speciality teas served with local treats – intriguing names include Cumberland rum nicky.

MARGARET'S TEA ROOMS
Chestnut Farmhouse, The Street, Baconsthorpe, near Holt, Norfolk; Tel 01263 577614
Everything is home-baked in this wonderful tearoom on the north Norfolk coast.

PEACOCKS
65 Waterside, Ely, Cambridgeshire; Tel 01353 661100
50 different teas, light meals and home-made cakes.

THE PUMP ROOM
4 Argyle Street, Bath, Somerset; Tel 01225 444477
Tea served in a magnificent room to music played by the Pump Room Trio or a pianist.

WADDESDON MANOR
near Aylesbury, Buckinghamshire;
Tel 01296 653242
Tea served in the old kitchen and
servants' hall of a National Trust house.

The following London hotels serve
excellent afternoon tea:

THE DORCHESTER
Park Lane, W1; Tel 020 7629 8888

THE FOUR SEASONS HOTEL
Hamilton Place, Park Lane, W1;
Tel 020 7499 0888

THE LANESBOROUGH
Hyde Park Corner, SW1;
Tel 020 7259 5599

THE RITZ
150 Piccadilly, W1;
Tel 020 7493 8181

Others places of interest:

ST JAMES'S TEAS LTD
5 Cobham Road,
Wimborne BH21 7PN;
Tel 01202 863806
This shop sells a wide range of
classic teas and runs educational
tea-tastings.

NORWICH CASTLE MUSEUM
Castle Meadow, Norwich;
Tel 01603 493648 (recorded information)
A good collection of teawares and a
gallery housing 3,000 teapots.

THE VICTORIA & ALBERT
MUSEUM
Cromwell Road, London SW7;
Tel 020 7942 2000
A fine collection of Oriental and
British tea bowls, tea cups, teapots
and silverwares.

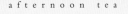

acknowledgments

The publishers would like to thank the following companies and individuals for the generous loan of photographic props for this book:

Bridgewater Pottery, London; Mark Buckingham/Justina Leitão; Erin Burnip; Chantry China, Andover; Dinghams Cookshop, Salisbury; Pam and David Pearson; Stiles of Alresford.

Thanks also to Lainston House, near Winchester, Hampshire, for allowing us to photograph on location, and to Viv Brett for her creative styling.

Photographs are reproduced by kind permission of the following:

Aurora: p30; His Grace the Duke of Bedford and the Trustees of the Bedford Estates: p25; Bramah Tea and Coffee Museum: p73; Bridgeman Art Library: pp10, 11, 14, 15, 16 (above), 17, 18, 33, 37, 63, 64, 71; Mary Evans Picture Library: pp8, 9, 19, 20, 21, 22, 23, 35, 36, 40, 41, 54, 56, 57, 59, 60, 61, 67, 70; Jarrold Publishing: p38; p62 (by Mark Buckingham); pp76, 77 (by Esther Gumn); pp47, 48, 49, 50, 51 (by Steve Morley); front cover, endpapers, pp1, 3, 26, 27, 28, 29, 34, 52, 53, 58, 64 (below), 74, 75 (by Neil Sutherland); LucileLtd (courtesy of Randy Bryan Bigham Esq): pp6, 55; National Portrait Gallery: p13; Robert Opie Collection: pp66, 68, 69; Period Living Magazine: pp6, 31, 32, 42, 43, 44, 45, 46, back cover; Carole Redlich: p72 (below); The Ritz Hotel, London: p39; Victoria and Albert Museum: pp12, 16, 24, 32, 65, 72 (above).